Writer, illustrator and outdoorsman, C. B. Colby speaks from wide personal experience whether writing about weapons, aviation or the outdoors. His articles have appeared in over twenty-five national magazines, and his nearly sixty books have covered almost as many subjects.

During World War II he served as a war correspondent and has traveled from Labrador to Mexico and from Alaska and Hudson Bay to the Caribbean for material for his writings and books.

He is a long time member of the Adventurers Club of New York, the Outdoor Writers Association of America, The American Ordnance Association, and was one of the founders of the Aviation/Space Writers Association. He has been an active member of Civil Air Patrol for over twenty years and holds the rank of Lieutenant Colonel.

Since he first learned to fly gliders in 1931 he has flown, or flown in, almost every kind of aircraft from gliders to jets and from bombers to blimps. His hobbies are camping, firearms, hunting and fishing.

Mr. Colby is married, has two grown children, and lives in Briarcliff Manor, New York.

CIVIL WAR WEAPONS

Small Arms and Artillery of the Blue and Gray

by C. B. Colby

Coward-McCann, Inc.   **New York**

Union Spencer Carbine with breech open. Below carbine is tubular magazine to hold cartridges. Above breech is rim-fire cartridge used in this weapon.

Contents

Full color cover transparency courtesy of National Park Service, Department of the Interior. U. S. Army photos from Army Picture Library: Title page; 3; 39; 40; 41; 42; 43; 44; 45; 47. Smithsonian Institution: 5; 7, bottom; 10; 11, third from bottom; 12; 15, bottom; 16; 20; 25; 27; 32. Colt Collection of Firearms: 21. Winchester Gun Museum: 8; 9; 11, top; 13, right; 14, next to bottom; 22, 25, 29, two center arms; 33; 35. Springfield Armory: 36; 37; 38, top. All others courtesy of Military Museum, United States Military Academy, West Point, N. Y.

Weapons of the Civil War

The tragic War Between the States was fought to determine the future of our great nation. During this devastating conflict, battlefields became vast and incredibly expensive testing grounds for weapons of all kinds.

From pikes and muzzle-loaders to Gatling guns, Henry repeaters and the giant "Columbiad" cannon, every type and make of weapon obtainable was put to use. Many proved to be excellent; some radical innovations were successes, others worse than useless, but from this tragic conflict, new and better weapons emerged to serve this nation well in later years.

The weapons used by both North and South were of many origins; some government issue, some homemade, some imported, some captured, and some reassembled from broken weapons picked up on the battlefield. Before open hostilities really began, government arsenals held over a half million muskets and about 50,000 rifles of various models and types. Vast stores of these were seized by the Confederacy when war broke out, but the North, with its great industry, had the edge in the manufacture of ammunition and arms, particularly the former.

During battles, arms were captured from both sides and used against the enemy in later conflicts. However, breech-loading weapons were of little or no value to the South in the early months of the war due to its lack of suitable ammunition for this type of weapon. Later the Confederacy manufactured its own breechloaders and ammunition for them.

At the onset of hostilities, Josiah Gorgas, Chief of Ordnance for the Confederacy, reported that the South had a total of about 143,000 serviceable arms, plus another 150,000 owned by state and county militia units. However, there was very little ammunition for these weapons. Ammunition was estimated at less than a million rounds in all the Confederate States. Even more desperate was the need for percussion caps with which to fire the pieces; hardly a quarter of a million caps in all were available.

However, American ingenuity as usual came to the rescue, and by 1863, with nearly a half million men under arms, the Confederacy had managed to equip them well.

In the North as well as in the South, it was difficult to obtain sufficient arms for the troops. Many units had to arm themselves from private funds. Some soldiers preferred to carry their personal weapons into action rather than use the often clumsy government-issue arms. Many times the contract weapons issued to troops proved to be quite unsuitable.

Agents from both the North and South were sent abroad to purchase weapons from European manufacturers, not only for use by their own troops but to keep the opposition from purchasing them. European arms manufacturers, not wishing to favor what might prove to be the losing side, sold to both sides with equal enthusiasm; often with more enthusiasm than integrity. They unloaded vast stores of obsolete and often unusable arms at high prices on the first agent to appear. They also turned out cheap imitations of good arms to profit by the sudden and desperate American markets.

Not only did some Northerners join the Confederacy to design and make arms for them, but some even made a profit from America's misery by running guns and ammunition to the South. Many a furious gun battle took place along our coasts between Union ships and gunrunners. Secretly, although glad to have their weapons, many a Southern gentleman looked with scorn upon these profiteering gunrunners.

The wide variety of weapons used, including the many copies of successful arms, the wild and weird experimental arms, the imports and the homemade weapons, makes it almost impossible to present a complete list of all types of Civil War weapons, no matter what the size of the volume. Even military historians often disagree as to which side used what, when they used it and where. Arms were taken from the dead and wounded on the battlefield and turned against the comrades of the fallen owners. Weapons were captured from armories and arsenals, confiscated from private homes and troop trains, bought from gunrunners and assembled from parts of broken firearms no longer serviceable.

After every battle vast quantities of arms were collected by the victor and sent to the rear for repair, reconditioning and reissue. Just how huge this reconditioning program was, carried out by both sides, can be demonstrated by the aftermath of a single battle. After the Battle of Gettysburg, over 35,000 rifles and muskets were collected and shipped to Washington for repair and reissue. What was found after inspection of these particular arms did much to change the course of weapons design from the muzzle-loader to the breechloader, a switch long advocated by many against stubborn government opposition.

Of the 35,000 arms collected on the battlefield from both sides, 24,000 were still loaded and nearly half of these had more than one charge superimposed on another in the barrels. Six thousand had as many as three to ten charges inside the barrel, and more than one had twenty charges inside. In the excitement and noise of the battle, soldiers on both sides had failed to notice that their weapons hadn't fired, so they had rammed another charge on top of the first and so on. Often a soldier had forgotten to put a percussion cap on the nipple at all, or had put the ball into the barrel first, followed by the powder charge, which prevented firing. Some who were using paper and linen cartridges had rammed them into the weapon wrong end first and couldn't remove them.

It was painfully evident, even to the stubborn advocates of the muzzle-loader, that a breechloader would eliminate such widespread mistakes, and so the swing to the breechloader began in earnest. After the Battle of Gettysburg, the U. S. Model 1863 rifled musket, already approved, was declared by the North the last of the muzzleloaders.

Both North and South were able to use weapons captured from the other side if they could obtain ammunition for them. Some weapons were used with makeshift ammunition; some were rebored or altered to accommodate what ammunition was available; others were stored until suitable ammunition could be manufactured or captured.

There were many ingenious arms designers on both sides of the struggle and they produced fine weapons, from pistols and shoulder arms to rapid-firing weapons and giant fieldpieces. Many makers of fine hunting rifles and superaccurate target rifles kept on making them for snipers and sharpshooters in the service of both sides. Many hunters-turned-soldiers preferred their accurate and lighter-weight hunting and squirrel guns to the heavier army-issue weapons, and many an owner of an accurate target rifle found himself assigned to sniper duty instead of fighting in the ranks.

In addition to the frantic manufacture of weapons for both sides, the capture of arms from the enemy often resulted in vast stores of serviceable arms. For example, the Confederates captured 35,000 U. S. Model 1861 rifled muskets at the Battle of the Wilderness; another 20,000 at the Second Battle of Manassas; 9,000 at Fredericksburg; 11,000 at Harpers Ferry and 15,000 more from Shiloh and Antietam; a total of 90,000 good weapons that could be turned against the North. Many weapons were in service on both sides several times through use, capture and reuse.

The Civil War, slow to start, soon involved all of America, with the tragic result that over 110,000 Union soldiers died in combat or from wounds, and 275,000 were wounded. The Confederacy lost 94,000 men; 150,000 were wounded. It is estimated that of all the men engaged in this titanic struggle, between 34 and 40 percent were either killed or wounded, a tragic and terrible price to pay to reunite the nation.

On the following pages you will find outstanding and interesting examples of the weapons used by both the North and the South in this great conflict. Some of these photos are of special historic interest, for they were taken by the famed Civil War photographer, Mathew Brady, using old glass plate cameras and crude equipment. Others are from such sources as the Military Museum at the United States Military Academy, West Point, N. Y., the Museum at the famed Springfield Armory, Springfield, Mass., The Smithsonian Institution, Washington, D. C., the Olin Mathieson Chemical Corporation Collection, the Colt Collection of Firearms and the U. S. Army Picture Library in Washington, D. C.

As usual, in doing research and collecting photos for such a book, I am indebted to many for their enthusiastic help and cooperation. I should like to thank the following in particular: Mrs. Donna Traxler, Chief, Army Picture Library; Mr. Ralph Anderson, National Park Service, Department of the Interior; Mr. Craddock Goins, Jr., Division of Military History, Smithsonian Institution; and Mr. Joseph P. Gannon, Supervisor of Special Services, Colt's Patent Fire Arms Mfg. Co. Inc. To Mr. Gerald C. Stowe, Curator of the West Point Museum, United States Military Academy, West Point, N. Y., my deep appreciation for his suggestions, enthusiastic help and contributions of both time and material. Matter of fact, I think I'd like to dedicate this book to "Jerry" Stowe, because of his enthusiasm for firing Civil War artillery, his love of the smell of black powder smoke and his pride in (and vast knowledge of) our early military history and military weapons.

To the Museum's Director, Col. Frederick P. Todd, as well, go my deepest thanks for his expert assistance and friendly cooperation.

On the following pages you will find over one hundred and twenty-five types of Civil War weapons from swords to siege guns. Tragic as was their use in the War Between the States, they helped forge our country into the great nation that it is, and helped make possible our vast military strength as a power for peace and a defense for the free world.

C. B. COLBY, Member
Company of Military
Collectors & Historians

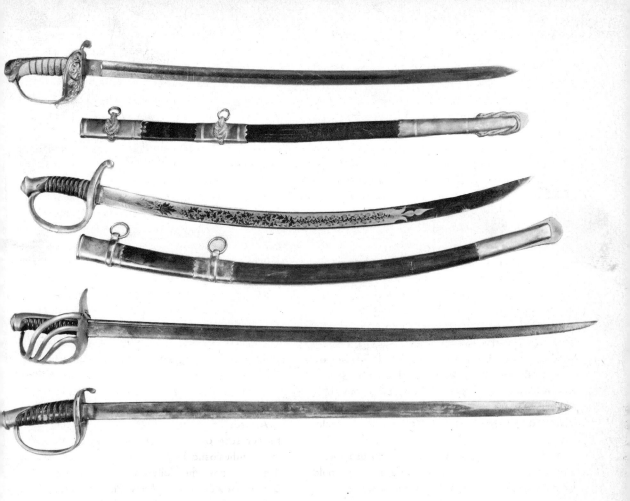

Confederate Swords

No longer generally used as weapons, swords were used during the Civil War by both officers and enlisted men as deadly arms in close combat. Today the wearing of the sword is reserved for dress and ceremonial occasions. Here is a representative collection of Confederate swords. From top to bottom: a Confederate Naval Officer's sword made by Robert Mole of Birmingham, England, and imported by Courtney & Tennant of Charleston, South Carolina; an Artillery Officer's saber with the traditional curved blade (note elaborate design on blade); a Cavalry sword marked *Texas*, which may mean that it was originally from the Republic of Texas; and a Confederate Foot Officer's sword made by Boyle, Gamble and Macfee of Richmond, Virginia. Note nautical knotted rope design on scabbard for top sword used by Naval Officer. Some of these had blades over a yard long.

Confederate Pikes

Ever since the days of the Homeric warriors and the Chaldean fighting men, 2000 B.C., soldiers have used sharp pointed and edged blades on long shafts. These have been called spears, lances or pikes. Some of the early Greek phalanx maneuvers used spears over twenty feet long. The Civil War pike was employed mainly by the Confederate States, for it could be manufactured quickly, cheaply and in great quantities using a minimum of vital metal. These pikes were usually on shafts from six to ten feet long and the blades were generally made of wrought iron. The designs were varied and each claimed to have special qualities that made it better suited for its purpose. From top to bottom in the collection shown above: a Confederate bridle-cutting pike with a hooked blade to sever bridles of cavalry horses; a "clover-leaf" pike; a Marschall Kane pike; and a sliding-blade pike. When not in use, this blade could be withdrawn into wooden shaft to protect blade from damage or to conceal it. Note ruler for sizes of blades.

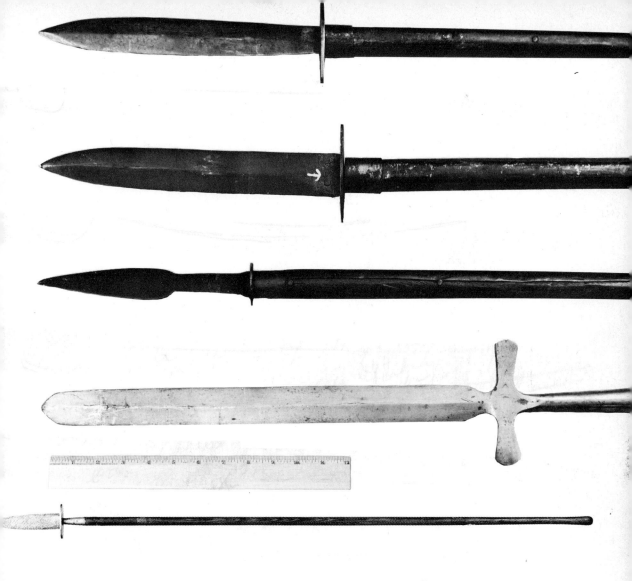

Georgia Pikes

Governor "Joe" Brown of Georgia was a great believer in the pike as a defensive weapon, and during the Civil War he ordered thousands of them manufactured for use against General Sherman's campaign. At top are four of the various types and designs turned out by several of his sources. John Brown (no relation) from Connecticut, who had a plan to arm Negroes and give them their own chance to fight for freedom, also designed and distributed many pikes. Full-length pike shown below pike tips is one of John Brown pikes picked up at Harpers Ferry, Virginia, after Brown staged an ill-fated attack. The battle took place at midnight, October 16, 1859, and resulted in the capture of Brown and seven of his men. Five others escaped and ten more of his followers were killed. Instead of aroused Negroes coming to join Brown's "cause," United States Marines appeared to arrest him for treason and murder in the first degree. He was later executed. His famous pikes are now museum exhibits. This one is in the famous Smithsonian Institution in Washington, D. C.

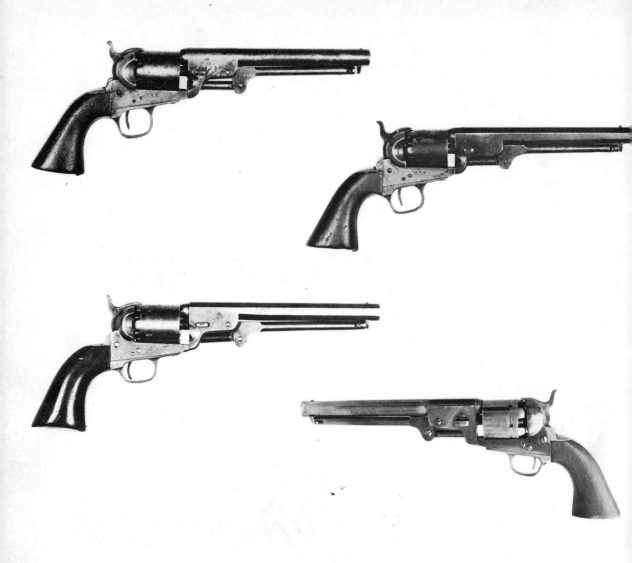

Confederate Revolvers

At the outbreak of the war, the Confederacy was without means to obtain weapons other than those that were already in their possession, or could be manufactured in the South. The inventiveness of Southern arms manufacturers came in good stead, and many fine examples of handguns or "side arms" began to appear. Here are some examples of these fine weapons turned out in the South. At the upper left is a Griswold & Grier percussion revolver made at Griswoldville, Georgia, 1862–1864. Its design closely duplicated the caliber .36 Colt Navy type so popular in the North. Known as the "Confederate Colt," it was the most famous C.S.A. (Confederate States of America) revolver; about 3,500 were made. This had a round barrel. Upper right is another of these fine revolvers with a regular Colt part-octagon barrel. Lower left is a fine Leech & Rigdon percussion revolver, also of .36 caliber. These were made by George Todd, who worked in Austin, Texas, 1857–1864, and Montgomery, Alabama, 1864. Lower right is another Leech & Rigdon handgun made at Greensboro, Georgia, in 1863. Also of .36 caliber and a very fine weapon.

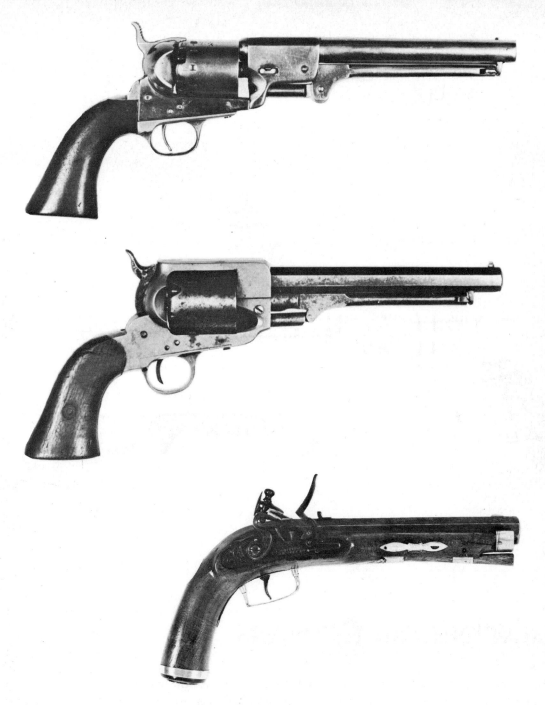

More C.S.A. Handguns

Here are three more interesting types of Confederate side arms. At the top is a Rigdon Ansley & Co. percussion weapon made in Augusta, Georgia, about 1864; a replica of the Colt Navy type revolver. The barrel is stamped C.S.A., and about 2,330 were made. Center photo shows a Spiller & Burr percussion revolver made in Atlanta, Georgia, 1863–1864. This is a replica of the Whitney Model revolver made at Whitneyville, Connecticut, in .36 caliber. About 1,400 of these were made. Bottom photo shows a handsome, silver-mounted flintlock pistol marked A. *Whiting* — *New Orleans*. This .46-caliber weapon was typical of many fine personal weapons used by some Confederates until they could obtain repeating firearms.

Imported Handguns Used by C.S.A.

Both North and South imported many firearms from Europe. Each side tried to prevent the other from making such purchases, often buying almost useless weapons to keep them from enemy hands. Here are some examples of European weapons used in action for the Confederacy. Top (this page), a British Adams percussion revolver imported in the early days of the war. Opposite page (top), a French Le Mat percussion revolver that was unique. It was of .38 caliber and fired nine shots from the cylinder and a 20-gauge shotgun charge from the barrel in the center of the cylinder below the regular barrel. (Front sight of this weapon is missing fom notch.) Second is a Kerr revolver patented by J. Kerr of England. This was a double-action (fired as fast as you pulled the trigger) arm of .44 caliber and carried five shots. Double-action handguns were in great demand. Third weapon is a French pin-fire revolver with a folding trigger and no trigger guard. Bottom photo is an English Adams five-shot double-action revolver of .44 caliber. This was particularly popular with the C.S.A.

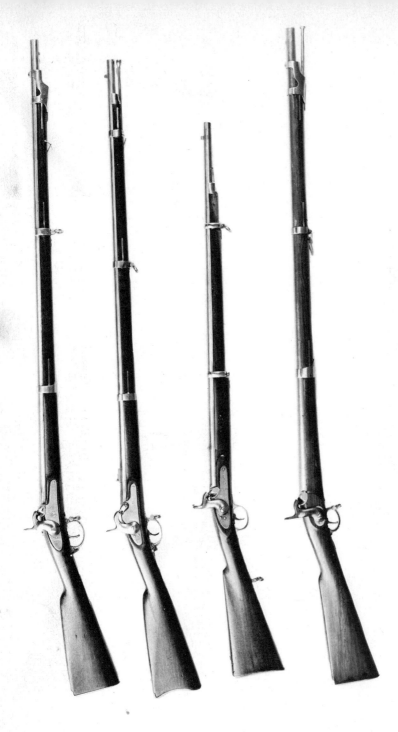

C.S.A. Percussion Shoulder Arms

The Southern gunsmiths turned out many fine weapons for the Confederacy, and here are four excellent examples of their skill. The first (left to right) is a Palmetto musket of 1852, made at the Palmetto Armory in Columbia, South Carolina, and modeled after the U.S. (Union) Model 1842. It was of .69 caliber and was smoothbore. Second is a Richmond rifled musket, about 1863, of .58 caliber. Third is a Confederate Cook infantry rifle of 1864. This was of .58 caliber and made in Athens, Georgia. Fourth weapon is made by George W. Morse in caliber .71, and of particular interest because the action is inside the wooden stock rather than attached to the outside.

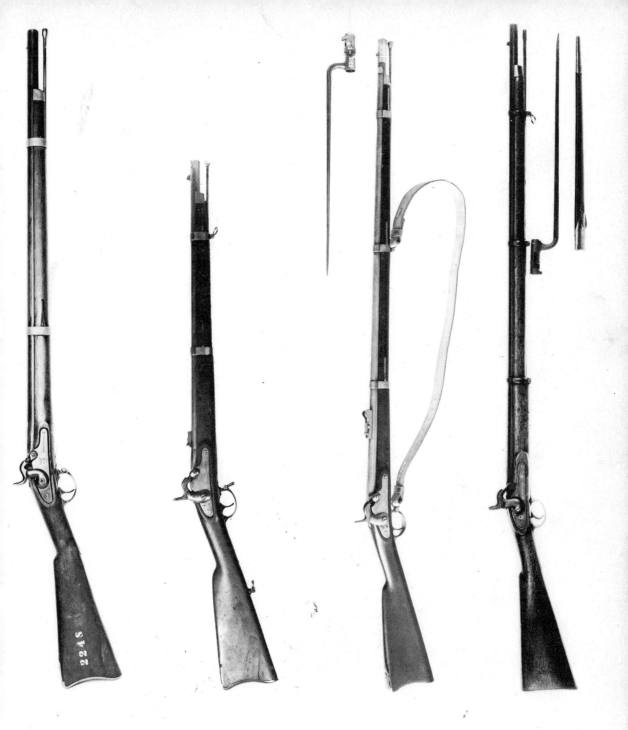

Four More C.S.A. Shoulder Arms

Four more fine examples of good gunsmithing. Left to right, a Fayetteville musket of 1864 made at Fayetteville, North Carolina; second, a Richmond "musketoon," a shorter version of the longer and more standard Richmond musket, third from left. These were both of .58 caliber and model 1863. Fourth is a Cook Brothers weapon modeled after the British Enfield. These were made in Athens, Georgia. The last two shoulder arms are shown with their bayonets. Cook Brothers weapon is shown with a bayonet scabbard for carrying the bayonet on the belt when not attached to muzzle of weapon. All bayonets were carried in scabbards when not on piece.

Carbines of the C.S.A.

The short-barreled carbine, easy to handle in brush or at close quarters, was a favorite with many troops of both Confederate and Union forces. Here are some examples of popular carbines used by the South. First (top to bottom) is a Confederate Sharps carbine of .52 caliber, made by S. C. Robinson Arms Manufacturing Co., Richmond, Virginia. Second, a Morse carbine in .50 caliber. Third, a Tarpley carbine in .52 caliber, fourth a Cook & Brother carbine made in Athens, Georgia, in 1864. The fifth weapon is a Confederate Perry carbine, .52 caliber, with a breech action similar to that of the Burnside breech action. It used a cartridge of rolled paper and linen.

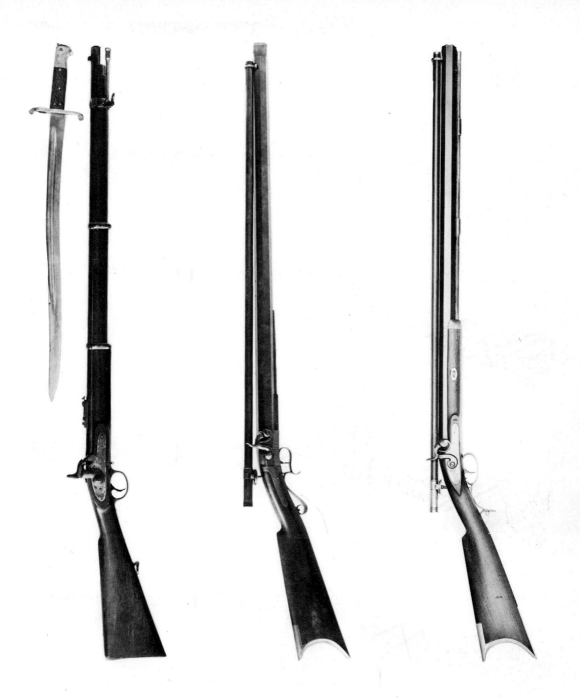

Confederate Snipers' Rifles

Both sides in the Civil War used snipers, expert marksmen with superaccurate rifles who concealed themselves in trees, upper windows and other places for the purpose of shooting unsuspecting pickets and other enemy troops. Many snipers used regulation weapons which had better than average accuracy, but the majority of them used (when they could get them) civilian target rifles with especially fine accuracy at many yards. Here are three examples of rifles used by Confederate snipers. At the left is an English Whitworth, caliber .45, which used a hexagonal bullet. Center rifle is a fine Morgan James target rifle and, like the civilian target rifle at the right, is equipped with a special long-range sighting tube.

15

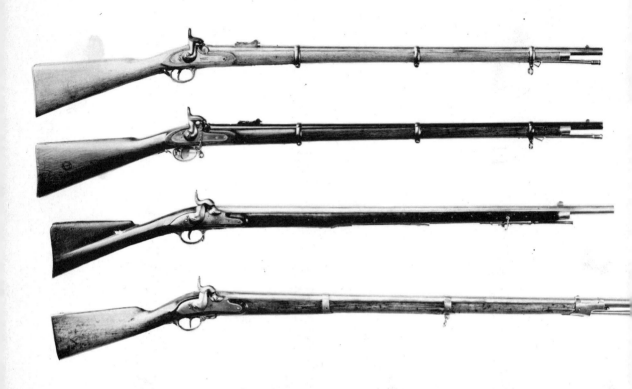

Imported Confederate Shoulder Arms

Here are some examples of excellent weapons imported by both the North and South, but used primarily by the C.S.A. First (top to bottom) is the Model 1858 British Enfield, considered by many to have been best of European weapons. The caliber was .577. More than 70,000 of these were purchased by the North and South before war was over. The second piece is a London Armory Enfield rifle, patterned after standard Enfield rifle, caliber .577. It was fitted with a chain-held nipple protector to prevent damage to the nipple when not in action. Third rifle is famous British Tower Musket, an obsolete flintlock converted to percussion firing system and purchased by the thousands. It was of .75 caliber. Fourth is a Prussian musket converted from flintlock to percussion, in caliber .69. It is interesting to note the overall similarity of these four different weapons and how closely they followed American designs.

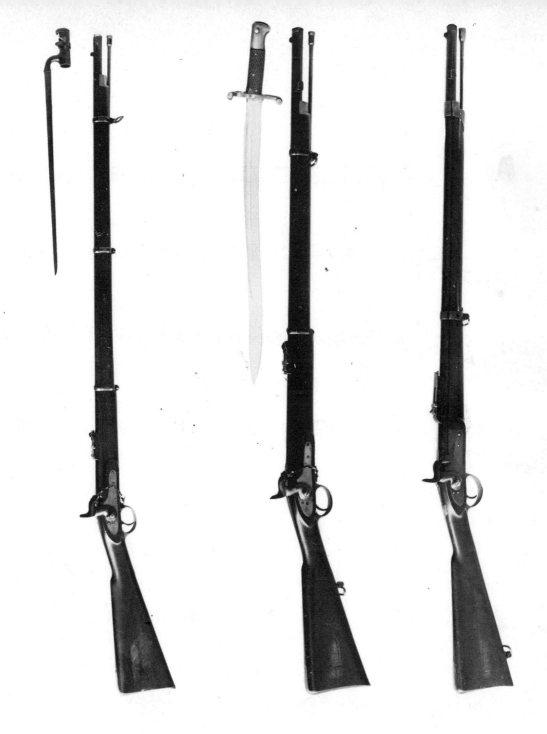

Three More C.S.A. Imports

Here are three more European weapons used by the Confederate States of America. Weapon at left is another version of the British Enfield, which, like the London Armory Enfield, also had a chain-held nipple protector. Some of these fine Enfields were elaborately finished with checkered stocks and fine-grain woods, for officers' use. This has typical triangular bayonet. Center weapon is another model of the British Enfield with a short barrel and used with a long sword-type bayonet which could also serve as a hand weapon. Right is Belgian percussion musket, caliber .58.

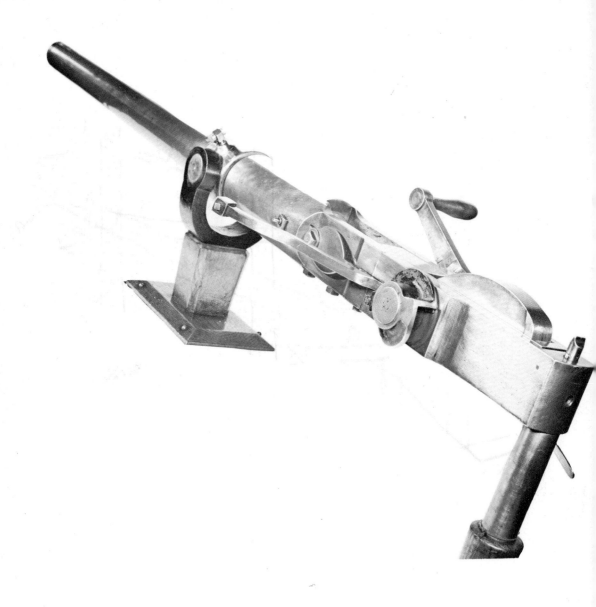

C.S.A. Williams Rapid-Fire Gun

This interesting rapid-fire weapon was designed by Captain R. S. Williams, C.S.A. of Covington, Kentucky. It was used at the Seven Pines, Virginia, battle, but wasn't too successful, as the breech expanded from heat of firing and failed to relock satisfactorily. It had a 1½-inch bore and fired a "spike-like" bolt, which was not only deadly but which emitted an uncanny screech when in flight, helping to unnerve the enemy. It was first tested on May 31, 1862, and was mounted on a two-wheeled carriage drawn by one horse. The Confederate Government ordered six of these interesting weapons to be built. The projectile weighed about one pound. This particular weapon is in the exciting Military Museum at the West Point Military Academy, West Point, N. Y., where many of these historic firearms are on display.

Gorgas Smoothbore Rapid-Fire Gun

Another interesting, experimental Confederate rapid-fire weapon was the Gorgas smoothbore piece, which was a sort of king-sized shotgun. It was designed by Major General Josiah Gorgas, C.S.A., class of 1841 at West Point. He was the Chief of Confederate Ordnance, and his weapon was a very interesting design. It had a rotating magazine which included eighteen copper-lined chambers, each fitted with a separate nipple. Charges were loaded into cylinder from outer rim opening near breech. This cast-iron weapon could fire either canister or solid shot. Canister shot consisted of many small bullets fired in a metal case which exploded at gun muzzle. Complicated mechanism made this weapon unreliable. Only a few made.

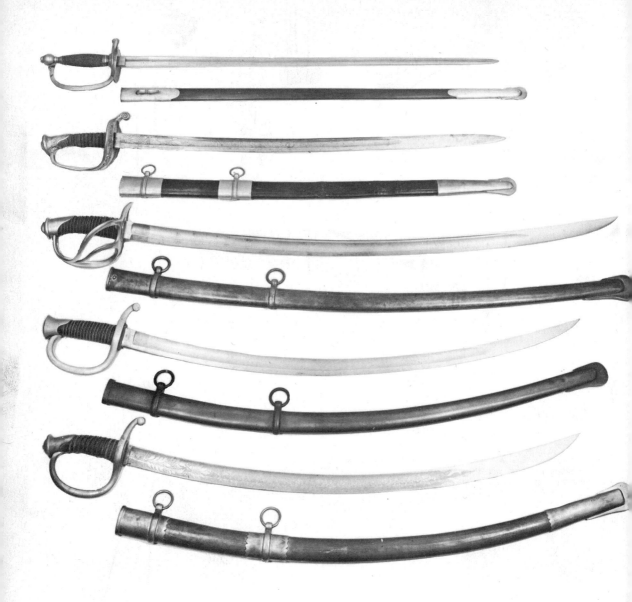

Union Swords

We'll begin the coverage of Union weapons in the same manner as the Confederate arms, with the swords. Both sides used swords more as symbols of rank than as weapons, except in close and desperate combat. They were usually drawn only by officers when advancing in battle. They were used to direct the action, or the flat side was applied to a scared or confused soldier to emphasize orders or directions. Here are five typical models of Union swords. From top to bottom: a Noncommissioned Officer's sword; a U. S. Foot Officer's sword; a U. S. Cavalry saber; a U. S. Artillery saber and a U. S. Artillery Officer's saber. Each is shown above its scabbard. Note that officers' swords were engraved while those of the enlisted men and noncommissioned officers were plain. The higher the rank of the commissioned officer, the more engraving on the sword. Cavalry troops were only units to use swords as standard weapons.

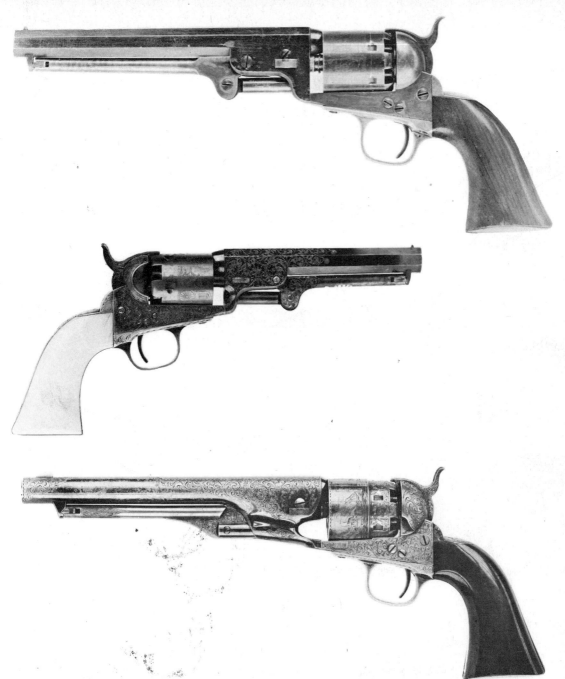

Union Colt Revolvers

Although many types of handguns were used by Union troops, the Colt revolver seems to be the one most thought of and written about. Here are three fine examples of both plain and engraved weapons by this famous manufacturer. At the top is a U. S. Navy Colt in caliber .36, Model 1851. It was a six-shot, single-action (hammer must be cocked before each shot) weapon, and was the property of Colonel J. L. Kerby Smith, Class of 1857, USMA, West Point. Colonel Smith died of wounds received at Battle of Corinth, Mississippi, October 12, 1862. Center weapon is an engraved 1849 Colt pocket revolver, and the bottom weapon is a Model 1860 Colt Army revolver in .44 caliber. This was presented to Major General George B. McClellan in 1860. Last two weapons are also single-action.

Union Colts With Stocks

For some assignments, troops carried stocks which could be attached to their revolvers, making them shoulder arms. Stocks gave better accuracy for long-distance shooting, yet could be removed quickly so the revolvers could be carried in belt holsters. Top to bottom: a 3d Model Dragoon Colt fitted with an 1855 U. S. type stock; a dragoon with another model stock giving more rigidity; and an 1860 Army Model .44-caliber revolver with one of these more rigid stocks. Each stock was fitted with a ring so it could be carried on a saddle or hung from the shoulder. Colt holster revolvers were usually all .36 caliber; pocket revolvers were usually .28, .31 or .34 caliber, and had shorter barrels.

Starr, Roger & Spencer, and Joslyn Revolvers

Many firearms manufacturers produced excellent weapons for the Union troops, even though in limited quantities. Here are three examples of such interesting handguns. First (top to bottom): a Starr six-shot Army percussion revolver of .44 caliber, which fired a self-consuming combustible cartidge. This weapon was particularly interesting in that it had two triggers; the larger one for double-action firing and the smaller, just visible at the rear of the trigger guard, for single-action firing. Second is a Roger & Spencer Army six-shot percussion revolver. This also was of .44 caliber, popular for military use. The third weapon was made by B. F. Joslyn and, like the others, was of .44 caliber. This five-shot weapon had an interesting side hammer mounted on the right side of the piece rather than in the center of the action.

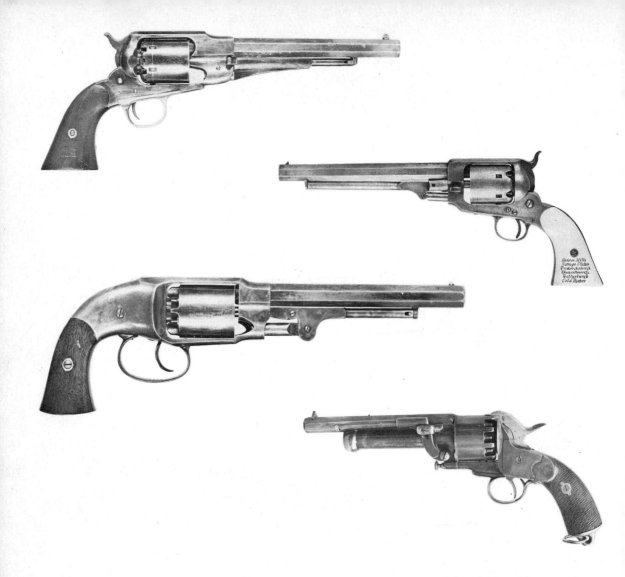

Remington, Whitney, Pettingill, and Le Mat Revolvers

Four famous names in arms manufacture are represented here. First (top to bottom) is a Remington Army New Model, caliber .44. Remington Arms contributed much to the early history of our country, along with Colt and other famous arms manufacturing companies. The second weapon is a Whitney Navy Model revolver in caliber .36. This was a single-action side arm owned by a Union soldier who carved the names of the battles in which he fought into the butt. Another list adorns the other side. The third weapon is an interesting Pettingill Army percussion revolver with a concealed hammer. This was a six-shot, double-action weapon of .44 caliber made by Rogers & Spencer. Fourth arm is the Le Mat revolver, which was also used by the C.S.A. This unique weapon was invented by Doctor (also Colonel) Alexandre François Le Mat of New Orleans, who moved to Paris, France, and had the weapon manufactured there. A huge handgun, it fired ten shots, nine of .44 caliber and one (through large smoothbore barrel under regular barrel) of .65 caliber. It also came in other calibers and gauges.

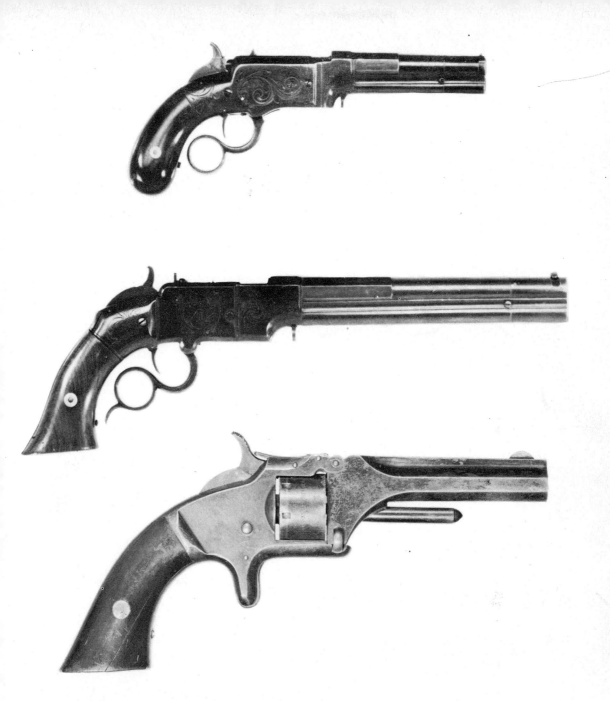

Smith & Wesson Weapons

First two weapons (top to bottom) are early Smith & Wesson arms of .31 (top) and .38 calibers. Both used the same lever action as that of lever-action repeating rifles. They were called "Volcanic Repeating Pistols" since they had no revolving cylinder found in true revolvers. They were a revolutionary design using self-contained cartridges and were the forerunners of the famous lever-action Winchester rifles. This unique type of weapon was introduced about 1854 and was the outgrowth of inventions by Walter Hunt, Lewis Jennings and Daniel Wesson, with Horace Smith. The third and smaller weapon is also a Smith & Wesson revolver, and was one of the first to use the rim-fire cartridges. It appeared in .22 and .32 calibers and was carried as a personal weapon by many Union soldiers and officers.

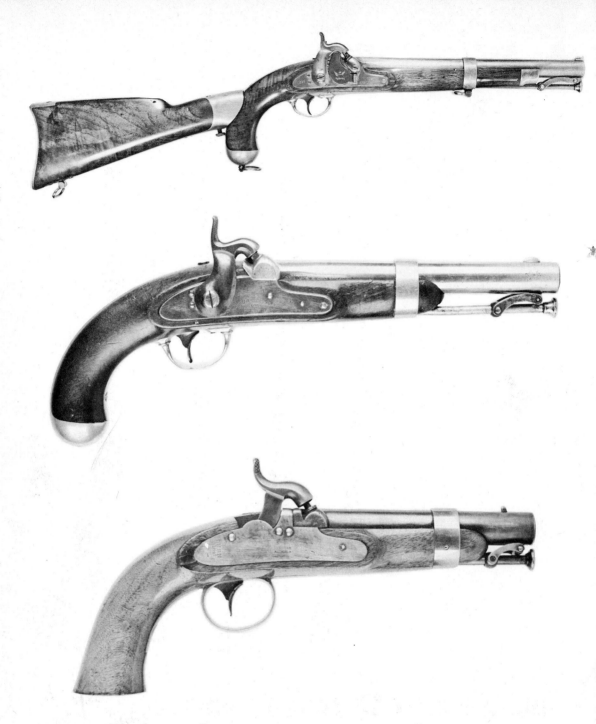

Muzzle-Loading Union Pistols

The desperate need for arms of almost any type forced the soldiers of both sides to use what otherwise might have been called obsolete weapons. The types shown above were used in vast numbers since great quantities of them were stored in armories around the country. At the top is a U. S. Springfield muzzle-loading percussion pistol-carbine of 1855, using a Maynard primer, invented by Edward Maynard. This was of .58 caliber. Center weapon is the Model 1842 U. S. Army muzzle-loading smooth-bore pistol manufactured by Aston in .54 caliber. The lower pistol was known as the U. S. Navy Deringer Model 1843. This was a small weapon of .54 caliber.

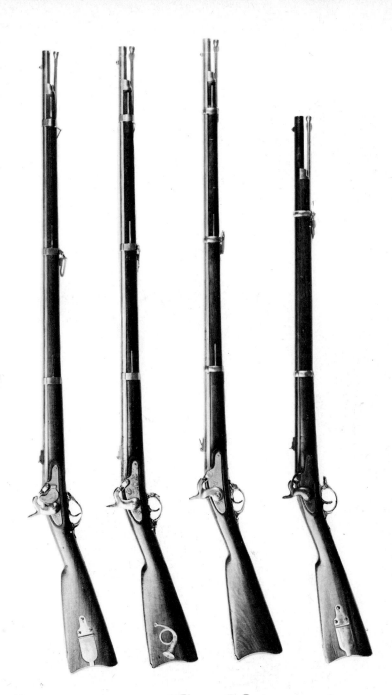

Four Union Percussion Shoulder Arms

These four fine examples of Union Civil War weapons include, left to right, a U. S. rifled musket, Model 1855. This weapon had a rifled bore and was made at Harpers Ferry Armory. Dated 1860, it was of .58 caliber, using the Maynard tape-primer system. Second is a Model 1861 rifled musket made at the famed Springfield Armory. This weapon was of .58 caliber. Third is a Model 1864 U. S. rifled musket of .58 caliber. This was the last of the muzzle-loading standard shoulder arms. Fourth weapon, with the shorter barrel, is a Remington Model 1862 rifle, known as the "Zouave Rifle" for its popularity with many militia units organized under the Zouave drill regulations during the Civil War. This was of .58 caliber also. Rifles at extreme left and right have brass patch boxes built into the butt of the wooden stocks.

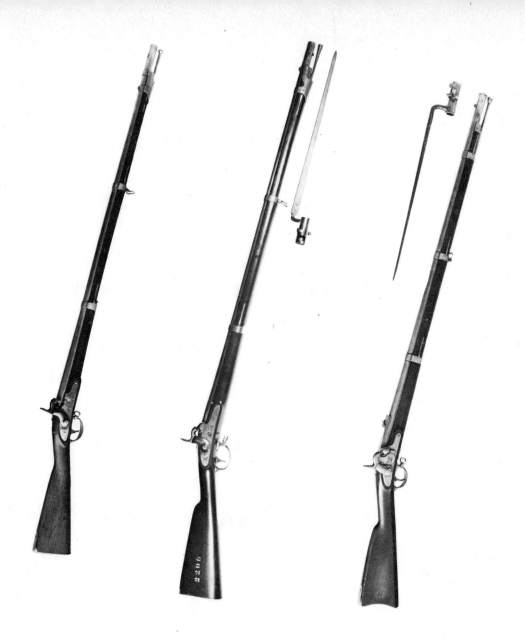

Three Types of the Famous Springfield

The famous Springfield Armory at Springfield, Massachusetts, turned out thousands of the above weapons for many years. At the left is a caliber-.69 Model of 1831 which was converted to percussion cap firing in 1843. Before then these weapons had used flintlocks for firing, but the percussion cap system became so popular that a majority of flintlock weapons were converted. You can see where the bottom of the "pan" had been removed from the side plate and a percussion cap nipple inserted into the barrel. The center weapon is a rifled musket of .69 caliber, also fired with a percussion cap. This was altered Model 1842 Springfield. The weapon at the right is Springfield equipped with a Maynard primer, Model 1855. This .58-caliber piece used caps in a paper tape instead of copper percussion caps. The caps unrolled from inside the Maynard primer unit just forward of the hammer. Weapons in center and at right are shown with their typical triangular bayonets.

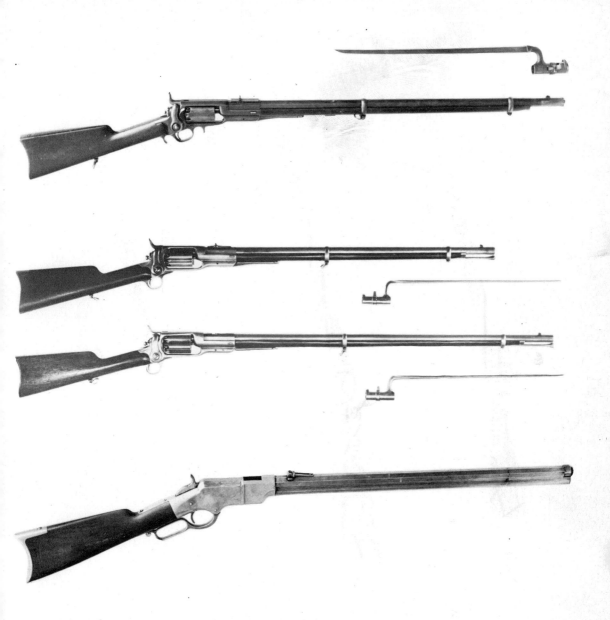

Union Repeaters

What every soldier wanted was a repeating rifle and many attempts were made to produce repeaters that were satisfactory. Here are some interesting types. Top three are Colt Revolving Rifles. They used the same cylinder type magazine as the Colt revolvers, enlarged to hold a bigger charge and bullet. They were made in long- and short-barrel models and were introduced about 1857. The top rifle was of .44 caliber and held six shots. This was called the Model 1855, even though it wasn't introduced until two years later. This type of weapon came in .36, .44 and .56 calibers. Later the side hammer was discontinued and the hammer located in the center as in the Colt revolver. The fourth rifle is the Henry magazine rifle, the forerunner of the Winchester carbine. It was of the 1860–1866 period and used rim-fire cartridges in .44 caliber. This was the beginning of a famous line of Winchester repeaters.

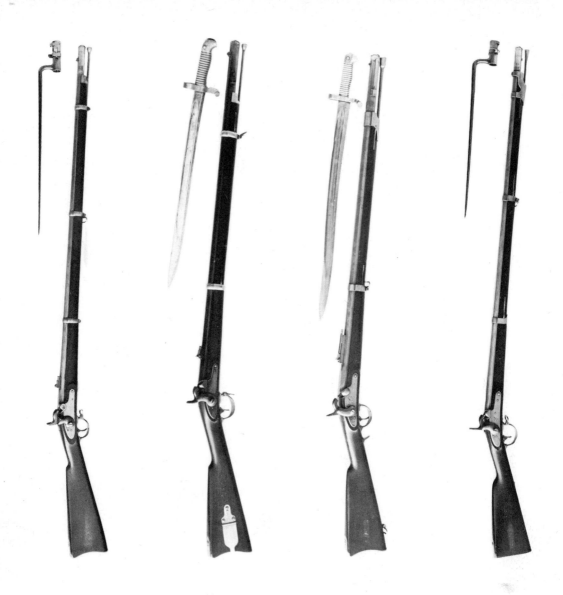

Muskets and Bayonets

This photo shows four Civil War muskets with bayonets used by Union forces. Many manufacturers, under contract, made weapons for the Federal troops, as you can see by the variety of makers represented here. The first (left to right) weapon was made at the Harpers Ferry Armory, a Model 1842 musket in .69 caliber with triangular bayonet. Second is a Remington percussion rifled musket, Model 1855 with a blade bayonet instead of the triangular type. The third is a Whitney percussion musket, caliber .58 and Model 1861, also fitted with a blade-type bayonet. The fourth weapon is a Colt musket, Model 1863, caliber. 58. All four weapons were fired by percussion caps and equipped with sling swivels. Each was loaded through the muzzle. They fired black powder and lead bullets, either round or conical shape, the latter called Minié balls. The Minié balls, a French invention, were far more accurate than the round balls and were used by both sides.

Union Arms from Europe

As already mentioned, the North, as well as the South, required so many weapons that they were forced to purchase quantities of arms from European suppliers. These weapons were bought from several countries, and many an exciting battle took place on the high seas off our coasts to capture the gunrunners taking weapons to both sides. Here are three types of foreign weapons used by the Union troops. Left to right, an Austrian muzzle-loading percussion rifled musket in .70 caliber, one of the largest calibers used. The middle weapon is a Prussian rifled musket, Model 1861. The weapon at the right is a German muzzle-loading percussion musket in .69 caliber. These German muskets were used in small quantities when no others were available.

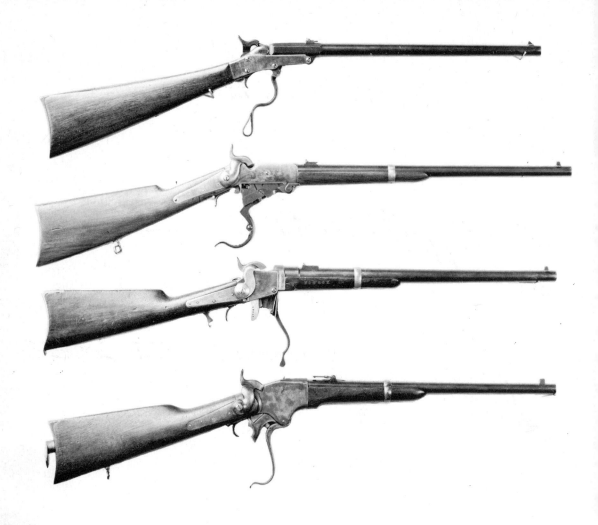

Maynard, Burnside, Starr and Spencer Carbines

One of the most popular weapons on both sides of the Civil War was the carbine, particularly valuable to the cavalry. Here are four outstanding types. First (top to bottom) is the Maynard breech-loading carbine in caliber .50. Below this is a Burnside breech-loading carbine. This interesting type used a brass cartridge which was dropped into the action butt first instead of bullet first. The breech was then raised with a lever placing the lead bullet of the cartridge into the barrel. It was invented by Amos E. Burnside, later a major general and commander of the Army of the Potomac. Third weapon is a Starr breechloader, patented in 1858 by Eben T. Starr, and using a linen cartridge fired by a percussion cap. Bottom carbine is a Spencer, patented in 1860 by Christopher Spencer. This used rim-fire cartridges of .52 caliber, fed into the breech from a tubular magazine in the stock. Seven cartridges could be carried in the magazine, and reloading was quick, making this carbine a very popular weapon. Both sides used these weapons whenever they could obtain them.

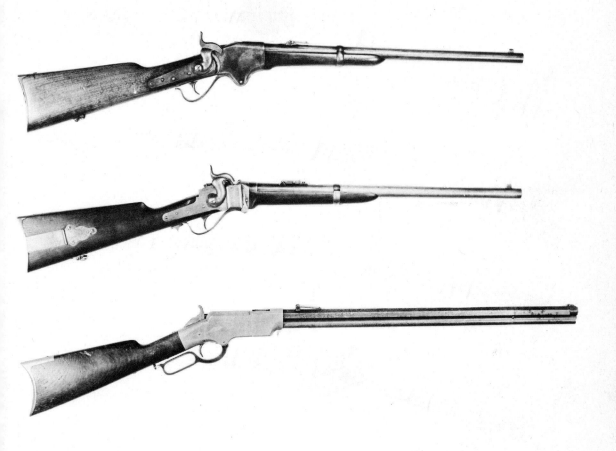

Spencer, Sharps and Henry Rifles

At the top is another photo of the Spencer shown on the opposite page, but with the action closed and tubular magazine fully inserted in butt. Below this is a Sharps carbine, one of the most famous of all Civil War weapons. (The word "sharpshooter," said to have originated because Civil War snipers used Sharps rifles, is actually a much older word with no connection to the Sharps rifle.) This was a .50-caliber breech-loader, Model 1848, with a brass patch box in stock. It used a pellet primer. Some later models used the Maynard primer system. Lower carbine is the repeating Henry rifle, forerunner of the Winchester carbine which is still one of the most popular hunting rifles. This was of .44 caliber. It is shown with other repeaters on page 29, but also belongs with the carbines. Long tubular magazine under barrel held the cartridges, sixteen in all. Confederate soldiers referred to the Henry as "that damned Yankee rifle that is loaded on Sunday and fired all week."

More Union Carbine Types

Top weapon is the Ball carbine, another fine breechloader. This was made by Ball & Lamson but usually referred to as the Ball carbine. It was of .56 caliber and used the Spencer rim-fire cartridge. This seven-shot weapon was little used. The middle weapon is a later version of the Sharps carbine using a metallic cartridge instead of the percussion type shown on page 33. Using metallic rim-fire cartridges, it required no patch box in the stock. This was Model 1863 and was of .52 caliber. Lower weapon is the Starr breech-loading carbine, also on page 32, but shown here with the cocking lever closed and the hammer at full cock ready to fire.

Four More Union Carbines

Carbines for Union troops were manufactured by several small manufacturers under contract. Here are four interesting models and makes. First photo (top to bottom) shows a Smith breech-loading carbine of .52 caliber, closely resembling the Ball carbine on opposite page. Second weapon is the Gallagher carbine in .54 caliber, with patch box in stock. Third is the Joslyn percussion carbine in .50 caliber, made by A. H. Waters & Co. This used a paper cartridge, as did the fourth weapon, a Union, or Cosmopolitan, breech-loading percussion carbine, in caliber .50.

14102 14102

Pre-Gatling "Coffee Mill"

Before Dr. Richard J. Gatling invented his famous gun in 1862, this rapid-firing weapon made its appearance in a skirmish along the Potomac that same year. The designer is still unknown, but the weapon was officially called the "Union Repeating Gun." It was of .58 caliber and, having only one barrel, it overheated quickly. It wasn't too successful since it had to be cooled before more firing. Due to its appearance it was known unofficially as the "Old Coffee Mill," which it resembled with the hopper on top (for cartridges) and a crank on the right-hand side. The cartridges were made of metal and contained a Minié ball, powder and a percussion cap. This rare weapon is in the Museum at the Springfield Armory in Springfield, Massachusetts. These pioneer rapid-fire weapons were considered almost as dangerous to the operators as to the enemy, so they were returned to the Washington Arsenal and scrapped. The boxes between the wheels, on either side of the gun, held ammunition and tools.

"Doctor Gatling's Rapid-Fire Gun"

The invention of a rapid-fire weapon by Dr. Richard J. Gatling revolutionized warfare to a considerable extent. These cleverly engineered weapons were made in several models and variations, all deadly. This .58-caliber weapon consisted of several barrels mounted on a wheeled carriage. Cartridges were fed by a hand crank to the barrels in turn, from a hopper above the breech. Most models had six barrels which fired in rotation. Since each barrel had a chance to cool between firings, the weapon could be fired for long periods without overheating. The rate of fire was fantastic, up to 800 shots a minute. Some later models had as many as ten barrels. Those slated for sea duty had barrels covered with a brass tube to protect them from salt spray. Some had shorter barrels and could be carried on horses or camel back. General Custer had several of these guns, but when he left for his final battle ("Custer's Last Stand") he left them behind because they were too much bother to carry. As the crank was turned, another barrel was revolved into place before the breech, a cartridge was inserted and fired, the empty shell extracted and another barrel rotated into position, etc. A remarkable weapon!

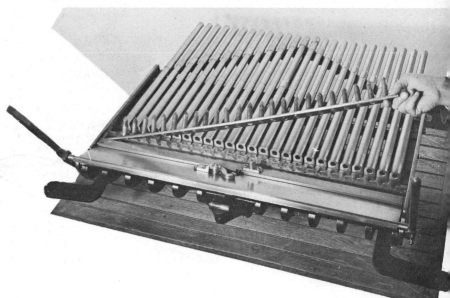

Requa "Eureka" Battery Gun

Billinghurst and Requa, a company experimenting with rapid-fire weapons, produced this sensational salvo gun. It fired twenty-five barrels at once in a deadly volley, used for protection of bridges and passes, or against closely packed enemy troops. It was of .52 caliber and all barrels fired at one pull of the lanyard. At first it used paper ammunition but later used metallic cartridges set into a perforated metal strip as shown in the lower photo. These strips were preloaded and inserted into the barrels and fired with one pull of the lanyard. It was simple in design, reliable (especially with the metallic cartridges) and heartily dreaded by the enemy. Upper weapon is in the Springfield Armory Museum and the lower model in the West Point Military Academy Museum at West Point, N. Y.

Seacoast Mortar and Defensive Mortar

Mortars were an important weapon for both sides in the Civil War. Here are two types of Union mortars. At the top is a huge 13-inch seacoast mortar mounted on a railroad flatcar. This giant weapon fired a round explosive shell which weighed 200 pounds for a distance of over 4,300 yards at a high angle. These were used against offshore ships and similar targets. The lower photo shows smaller mortars of 8- or 10-inch bore mounted on iron beds. These were photographed at Sullivan's Island, Charleston Harbor, S. C. Note demolished buildings in background. Mortars fired their projectiles at a high angle to clear obstructions which were in front of them or which protected the enemy from more direct fire.

Stockpile of Mortars

This historic Mathew Brady photo, taken in 1864, shows lineup of equipment stored at City Point, Virginia, and used by General Ulysses S. Grant during his campaigns in the South. In the foreground are piles of mortar shells, behind which are rows of 10- and 13-inch Union mortars. The guns in the background are Parrott Rifles mounted on wheeled carriages. Note the sailing ships in the background and the barges used to handle heavy artillery. Smaller mortars are in nearest row to the right, behind seated soldiers.

10-Pound Parrott Rifle and Bronze Gun Howitzer

These two rare photos of Civil War artillery show, top, a battery of 10-pound Parrott Rifles (cannon) at the Battle of Seven Pines in 1862. These rifles were designed by Robert Parrott, who placed heavy wrought-iron bands around the breech of the cannon for more strength at the point of greatest strain. This made the weapon much stronger and able to use heavier charges of powder for longer range and better penetration. They came in seven sizes; from ten-pounders (shown above) to 300-pounders. These figures represent weight of projectile. A group of the larger Parrotts hammered Fort Sumter to pieces from two miles away! Lower photo shows a 12-pound bronze gun howitzer, known as a "Napoleon," with its battery squad. This squad was composed of six men, each with a specific duty to perform during firing and reloading. These bronze howitzers could fire two aimed shots a minute with shells or solid balls, or four canister charges at point-blank range, requiring no aiming.

12-Pound Boat Howitzer

This rare photo shows a 12-pound bronze boat howitzer, called the Dahlgren, on the deck of the Union *Monitor*. It was invented by John A. Dahlgren and used primarily by the Union Navy. It fired an explosive 12-pound shell and could be moved about on its metal wheeled carriage. The gun crew members are posed in position for firing the piece (note raised hand of the man in the left rear). This historic photo is of special interest because of the various dents in the turret of the *Monitor* in the rear, quite possibly put there by the Confederate *Merrimac* during their historic battle, March 9, 1862.

20-Pound and 30-Pound Parrott Rifles

These two larger Parrott Rifles are shown during drills by Union gun squads. The top photo shows a 20-pound Parrott and its crew ready to fire. Note man at right pulling lanyard. The crew for this size cannon consisted of seven men working as a team. Note man at left with sponge on ramrod. This was dipped in bucket of water (under cannon) and used to swab the bore after each firing to quench any sparks left burning from last charge. This prevented fresh powder charge from exploding as it was inserted. Hot barrel evaporated water before a fresh charge was inserted. Lower photo shows a group of the heavier 30-pound Parrotts behind log-and-sandbag parapet and mounted on siege carriages. The two men standing by trailpiece are holding long tools in their hands called "handspikes." These are ironshod wooden crowbars used to move the trail of the carriage from side to side for aiming cannon. Crewman at right holds sponge.

32-Pound and 42-Pound Cast-Iron Guns

Here are two sizes of heavy cast-iron, smoothbore guns on front-pintle wooden Barbette carriages. These carriages were designed by a Frenchman named de Gribeauval in the eighteenth century. They enabled a cannon to fire over a parapet instead of through openings called "embrasures." The back of the carriage moved left and right on wheels set on a track, while the front of the gun pivoted on a stout peg or "pintle." Note wheels under rear of these cannon and wooden tracks. Top photo also shows pile of grapeshot projectiles by front wheels. These projectiles separated upon firing, spraying balls among troops. The big wooden wheels permitted movement of cannon when removed from Barbette carriage. Top gun is 32-pounder and lower photo shows 42-pounder.

100-Pound and 200-Pound Parrott Rifles

The larger Parrott Rifles were mounted on iron Barbette carriages instead of wooden ones. They also had front pintle as pivot. Top photo shows a 100-pound Parrott on such a mount. Note reinforcing bands around breech. Guns in rear are smaller Parrotts mounted on wheeled carriages. Lower photo shows a 200-pound Parrott, also on a front-pintle iron Barbette carriage. Note larger crews required to service these larger weapons, and circular track enabling gun to be rotated to fire in a 360-degree range. Lower photo is of gun installation at Missionary Ridge, Tenn.

150-Pound Armstrong Cannon

This huge cannon, mounted on a wheeled carriage at the United States Military Academy at West Point, N. Y., is a 150-pound (projectile weight) Armstrong iron cannon. Note reinforcing bands encircling barrel to give additional strength around breech. Lower photo shows rear of this huge cannon and ratchet device for raising breech to change aim. In the upper photo note two metal stubs protruding from the sides of the muzzle. These were supports for a wooden muzzle plug called a "tampion," which was used to keep out moisture and such occasional intruders as birds or rubbish. The small wheels under the heavy mount of this cannon permitted it to move backward along the flat rails from recoil. The lower wheels of the carriage permitted swinging from side to side to cover wider field of fire.

15-Inch Rodman "Columbiad"

About the largest cannon used during the Civil War was the "Columbiad," developed by Colonel George Bomford, U.S.A., and further developed by T. J. Rodman in 1860. This was a huge weapon with a bore of 8, 10, 15 or 20 inches. The top photo shows a 15-inch Rodman Columbiad mounted in a fort on a center-pintle iron carriage. This monster fired a 330-pound projectile to 1,518 yards at average elevation, or to 5,000 yards at a greater gun elevation. The 20-inch Columbiad had a barrel which weighed 54 tons. These guns were made by casting the barrel around a water core so that the inside of the barrel cooled first, and was then compressed by the cooling of the outer metal. Guns made in this way could withstand great pressure without bursting from charges needed to heave the huge projectiles for great distances. (Projectile for 20-inch model weighed 1,000 pounds.) Today two of these great guns can be seen, one at Fort Hancock, N. J., and one at Fort Hamilton, Brooklyn, N. Y. Lower photo shows one of these great Columbiads being drawn by eighteen oxen to protect Washingon, D. C., in 1864. Note, in upper photo, sponge, rammer and tampion. Holes in carriage wheels are for levers used to help move gun on track.

Arsenal Models

One of the problems of gun manufacture during Civil War times was the fact that few workers in gun factories could read or follow blueprints. The solution was to first make a perfect scale model of the weapon to be manufactured. These models were exact in every detail right down to ropes, tools, bolts and nuts and fittings. All the arsenal workers had to do was use the same materials and make each part as many times larger than the model as was required for the full-sized weapon. Many of the beautiful scale models for early arsenal workers can be seen at the West Point Military Museum at West Point, N. Y. At the top is an arsenal model of a brass Civil War fieldpiece, and below this, two models of mortars, the one on the right complete with miniature bucket and tools. Note also the completeness of detail in the top model, with its caisson for carrying ammunition and other gear. Workmen who were unable to read or write their own names could "read" such detailed models as these with ease, and turn out full-sized weapons, perfect in every way.